Near Water

Honor Head

WAYLAND

Explore the world with **Popcorn** - your complete first non-fiction library.

Look out for more titles in the **Popcorn** range. All books have the same format of simple text and striking images. Text is carefully matched to the pictures to help readers to identify and understand key vocabulary.
www.waylandbooks.co.uk/popcorn

First published in 2009 by Wayland

Copyright © Wayland 2009

Wayland
338 Euston Road
London NW1 3BH

Wayland Australia
Level 17/207 Kent Street
Sydney NSW 2000

Editor: Jean Coppendale
Designer: Alix Wood
Picture research: Taglines Creative Limited

British Library Cataloguing in Publication Data:
Head, Honor
    Near water. - (Popcorn. Watch out!)
    1. Drowning - Prevention - Juvenile literature
    I. Title II. Series III. Near water
    363.1'23-dc22

ISBN 978 0 7502 5790 9

Printed and bound in China

Wayland is a division of Hachette Children's Books, an Hachette UK Company.
www.hachette.co.uk

Photographs:
Cover, 4, Mike Booth/Alamy; 5 Juriah Mosin/Shutterstock; 6 Losevsky Pavel/Shutterstock; 7 Olga Lyubkina/Shutterstock; 8 Tischenko Irina/Shutterstock; 9 Lisa Thornberg/istock; 10 JJpixs/Shutterstock; 11 Anyka/Shutterstock; 12 JHDT Stock Images LLC/Shutterstock; 13 Jamie Grill/Getty; 14 Brykaylo Yuriy/Shutterstock; 15 Neale Cousland/Shutterstock; 16 Sheldon Levis/Alamy; 17 Gelpi/Shutterstock; 18 PhotoSky 4tcom/Shutterstock; 19 Olga Lyubkina/Shutterstock; 20 Vera Bogaerts/Shutterstock; 21 Jim West/Alamy.

Contents

Water fun

Playing in water and learning to swim is fun. Always tell an adult when you are going in the water.

Always use armbands when you are learning to swim.

You cannot breathe under water
so you need to be careful when
you are in or near water.

The water in
a pond can
be very deep.

Walking near water

Going for walks is good for you. If you are walking near water make sure you have an adult with you.

Always stay close to an adult when you are near water.

When you play by a lake make sure someone is with you. Be careful not to fall in. The water in a lake might look calm but it could be moving very quickly.

Never swing over water from tree branches or ropes.

Streams and rivers

The water in streams and rivers can be very deep. Stay away from the edge of the river as it could be muddy and slippery.

A river can look calm but still be dangerous.

Fishing is fun but always stay on the bank. Take your fishing equipment home with you when you leave.

These children are wearing life jackets to keep them safe if they fall in.

Dirty water

Stream and pond water can be dirty even if it looks clean. Never ever drink from a stream or a pond because it can make you sick.

Take plenty of drinking water with you if you are going out for a long time.

Cover any cuts on your hands or feet
before you go into water. If you don't,
the cuts could become infected and sore.

A waterproof
plaster keeps
cuts clean
when you are
near water.

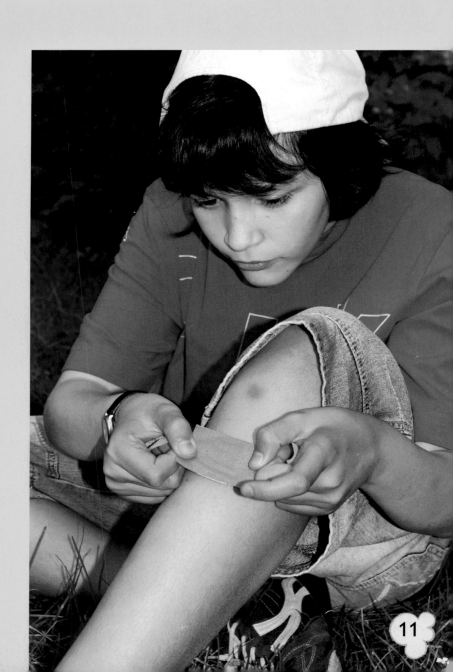

11

 Rubbish

Watch out for rubbish in the water.
If there is any rubbish, stay away!

Broken glass, rusty tin cans
and bits of metal can cause
nasty cuts.

Never throw rubbish into streams, lakes or ponds. Take it home or put it in a rubbish bin.

Only pick up rubbish if you know what it is and never touch needles or glass.

At the seaside

Paddling in the sea is fun but make sure an adult is watching you. The sea is always moving and could pull you away from the beach.

At the seaside look out for a red and yellow flag. This shows you where it is safe to play and swim in the water.

When the red and yellow safety flag is flying, it is safe to go in the water.

Stay with your friends or family on the beach and in the sea.

At the swimming pool

Swimming is fun and good exercise. At the swimming baths never run around the pool or in the changing rooms. You could slip and hurt yourself.

If you are not swimming stay away from the edge of the pool.

Armbands, swim rings and floats
help to keep you safe in the water.
You should use these until you are
a good swimmer.

Armbands keep you
afloat in the water.

Never jump on
other people or
push them into
the water.

Boating

If you go out in a boat, always make sure that an adult is nearby. If you are boating when it is cold, remember it can be much colder on the water than on the land.

Wear sunblock if you are sailing when it is warm.

Life jackets are filled with air and keep you afloat. You always need to wear a life jacket if you go out in a canoe or a boat.

Why do you think a life jacket keeps you safe?

Ice

When it is very cold, the water on ponds and lakes can freeze and become ice. Ice is slippery and cracks easily. Never walk on frozen ponds or lakes.

When lakes are frozen, you cannot tell how thick the ice is.

If you want to ice skate, go to a proper ice skating rink. It is a good idea to wear gloves and warm clothing when you are skating.

Gloves will stop your hands from getting hurt if you fall.

What's safe and what's not?

Match a sentence with a picture to see what is safe and what isn't when you are near water. Answers on page 24.

1. Before you go in the water, cover any cuts with a plaster.

2. Until you learn to swim always wear armbands.

3. On the beach, look out for the safety flag.

4. Never walk on a frozen lake or pond.

5. Wear a life jacket to keep you safe on the water.

6. Enjoy walks by the water but go with an adult.

Glossary

boating   going on the water in a boat or canoe

calm   when the water looks flat and smooth. Water can look calm on top but be moving very fast underneath.

infected   this happens to a cut when it becomes dirty or is not kept clean. When a cut is infected it takes longer to heal and can be very sore.

life jacket   a special jacket filled with air that you wear over your clothes. If you fall in the water it keeps you afloat.

sunblock   a cream that stops the sun burning your skin

waterproof plaster   a special plaster that keeps a cut dry

Index

Answers to puzzle: 1e, 2b, 3d, 4c, 5a, 6f